Child's Guide to the Mass

SUE STANTON

ILLUSTRATIONS BY
H. M. ALAN

PAULIST PRESS
New York / Mahwah, N.J.

Caseside illustration by H. M. Alan
Caseside design by Robin Doane

Stanton, Sue, 1952-
    Child's guide to the Mass / by Sue Stanton ; illustrations by H. M. Alan.
       p. cm.
    ISBN: 0-8091-6682-8 (hardcover)
       1. Mass—Celebration—Juvenile literature. [1. Mass—Celebration. 2. Catholic Church—Liturgy.] I. Alan, H. M., ill. II. Title.

BX2230.2 .S73 2000
264′.02036—dc21

                                                              00-057452

Published by Paulist Press
997 Macarthur Boulevard
Mahwah, New Jersey 07430

www.paulistpress.com

Printed and bound in Mexico.

To Dismas:
Thank you for the example
of your great love for liturgy.
—Sue Stanton

In loving memory of
Ella Diana Pilcher Hicks.
For Kaitlin, Delaney,
Kade K., and Karen S.
—H. M. Alan

Hi! My name is Sarah. I'd like to invite you to be with me and my family at church today. There is a special Mass this morning for children. What's a Mass? I'll show you.

"Hi, Josette. What are you doing?"

"I'm a greeter. I welcome people as they come into church. I give them a copy of a special booklet, or program. Inside there are prayers and songs that we will be using." **Look at the picture Luis drew for the program cover.**

We'd better go in and get a seat. We like to sit in the front.

"Good Morning, everyone! Welcome to the Children's Mass. Today's Gospel tells us about the time Jesus encouraged his friends to shine like a light for all the world to see. They could shine by using the talents God gave them, sharing their faith and helping others. All of us are friends and disciples of Jesus. We need to shine as well."

GOOD NEWS

I think Mass is getting ready to start. Let's listen to Melissa.

Now we sing the *Gathering Song*. It begins the first part of the Mass called the *Introductory Rite*. Doesn't the choir sound great? Maybe I will sing in the choir someday! Father Mike is coming into the church. **Can you see him singing?**

Can you find?

"Good morning, everyone!"

Father Mike invites us to join together and praise God. Jillian and Rajan stay near the altar throughout the Mass with Father Mike. They are called *Servers* or *Acolytes*. They wear long robes and help Father Mike when he needs them.

When I'm older, I'd like to be a server. Would you?

Father Mike leads us in the *Penitential Rite*. He says a prayer and we say, "Lord or Christ, have mercy."

When we are truly sorry, God forgives us. I use this prayer a lot! **Do you have a special prayer?**

The next part of the Mass is called the *Liturgy of the Word*. The *First Reading* is often read from a part of the Bible called the *Old Testament*. The Old Testament is a group of books that were written a long time ago. **Can you see the words *Old Testament* on Melissa's Bible?**

Our choir leads us in praying a *Psalm*. The choir sings the words of our prayer first, then we sing a response. Whenever I sing the Psalm response, I try to imagine how the first Christians sang many years ago.

The *Second Reading* is taken from the *New Testament*. The New Testament is filled with stories about Jesus and his friends. It is often a letter encouraging people to follow Jesus. **Can you find a shining light?**

After the Second Reading, Father Mike reads the *Gospel*. The Gospels are the most important part of the Liturgy of the Word. The word *gospel* means "good news" because these writings are the wonderful news Jesus brought to the world. **Can you find the banner we made that says *Good News*?**

To help us find Jesus' message, Father gives a *Homily*. During the homily, Father speaks about the meanings of the readings we just heard.

After Father's homily, we stand to say a prayer. It is called the *Profession of Faith*. We say this prayer with all our heart because in it we list many of the things that we believe about our relationship with God. **Can you say this prayer by heart?**

Next are the *General Intercessions*, or the *Prayer of the Faithful*. We ask God to help our parish family, our church family, and everyone throughout the world. Some of my brother's friends are reading prayers. **Do you have any prayers you'd like to say?**

There are times when the General Intercessions can also mean doing acts of kindness for others. Sometimes we have a special basket to collect food for people who do not have enough to eat. **Can you find the basket of food?**

The organist helps us by sharing her musical talents with us. There are many people who care in our church.

Now begins the *Liturgy of the Eucharist*. This is a special meal we will share together. Everyone helps out, just like we do at home. One family brings bread and wine to the altar. Father blesses it. He prepares the meal in the same way that Jesus prepared a meal for his friends when he wanted them to know how special they were to him. It is very quiet in church now. It is a holy time.

Father Mike begins to say the *Eucharistic Prayer*. He speaks the words Jesus said to his friends: "Take this all of you and eat. This is my body given up for you." Then Father Mike takes the cup of wine and says, "Take this all of you and drink. This is the blood of the new and everlasting covenant. Do this in memory of me." Now the bread and wine become the body and blood of Christ, even though they still look the same. This is called the *Consecration*. Jesus is with us. **Close your eyes and think about Jesus.**

Father Mike continues to pray. He prays for the church's leaders and for all those who have died. I feel good knowing that this is a time for me to remember my grandma and grandpa.

We say together as one family around the table the prayer that Jesus said.

Our Father, who art in heaven, hallowed be thy name; thy kingdom come; thy will be done on earth as it is in heaven. Give us this day our daily bread; and forgive us our trespasses as we forgive those who trespass against us; and lead us not into temptation, but deliver us from evil. Amen.

It is time for the *Sign of Peace*. Father Mike comes over to me. "Peace be with you, young lady," he says. "Peace to you, too, Father." Father Mike and I shake hands. Now I have to pass it on, so I shake hands with the lady next to me. Sometimes I wish the whole world could give one another a big handshake of peace. **How many people can you shake hands with?**

Even though I am not old enough to receive *Communion*—another name for the consecrated bread and wine—I always stand with my parents in the Communion line. But, guess what? Father Mike places his hand on my head and gives me a special blessing! I like that, but I still can't wait to make my *First Communion*.

Mass is just about over. Father gives Communion to *Eucharistic Ministers* who will take it to the people in the parish who aren't able to come to church, like the sick and elderly. **How many Eucharistic Ministers do you see?**

Father Mike blesses us by making the *Sign of the Cross*. **Can you draw the sign over Father's hands?**

"Go now and bring the light of Jesus to everyone you see."

The music begins and the choir sings. I sing, too!

Father Mike and the servers are the first to leave. I can tell that Father Mike likes this song. **Can you tell?**

He will be waiting to greet us at the back of the church when we get there. He shakes everyone's hand . . . even the babies'!

After Mass, we gather outside. Mom and Dad speak to their friends and I get to play with mine for a while.

Our church is a home away from home. Our parish is our family.

I'm glad you were here with me to share in our family and in the Children's Mass. I'm going to show my special light to everyone I meet this week. **Will you?**